On Shifting Shoals

On Shifting Shoals

Poems by

Joanne Durham

Cover design by Shay Culligan
Cover image by Joanne Durham

ISBN: 978-1-63980-150-3

Kelsay Books
502 South 1040 East, A-119
American Fork, Utah 84003
Kelsaybooks.com

This book is dedicated to everyone who never tires of the ocean, especially the Mylies III, IV, and V, Rachel, and Olive

Acknowledgments

Many thanks to the editors of the following publications, electronic and traditional, where these poems first appeared, sometimes in slightly different versions.

Evening Street Review: "The Leap"

Eunoia: "After the House Fire"

Gyroscope: "Words Matter—Choose Wisely"

Hole in the Head: "The Senior Citizen and the Boy Scout"

Kosmos Quarterly: "Garbage"

Poetry East: "A Father Teaches His Daughter to Ride the Waves"

Poetry in Plain Sight (North Carolina Poetry Society): "Words"

Quartet: "You Can't Put the Red Sea in a Poem"

Third Wednesday: "Christmas Tree Recycled in the Dunes"

Tipton Poetry Journal: "Bluefish Lane"

Verse Virtual: "Carnival," "Sand Stories"

Your Daily Poem: "Rescue," "Recipe"

Special thanks to everyone who has helped me grow as a poet through workshops, critique groups, prompt groups, and the patience and love of family and friends. You are too many to mention, but I thank you all.

Contents

Sand Stories 13

A Father Teaches His Daughter
    to Ride the Waves 14

The Hunt 15

Orange Butterflies/Orange Blossoms 16

Rite of Passage 17

Bluefish Lane 18

Words Matter: Choose Wisely 19

Rescue 20

Waiting for the Coronavirus 21

The Mayor Supports Oil Drilling off Our Coast 22

Words 24

The Leap 25

After the House Fire 26

The Senior Citizen and the Boy Scout 27

America 28

Phone Conversation with My Husband about Our
    Final Resting Places 29

Ghost Crabs on the Beach at Night 31

Last Year for the Carnival at the Beach 32

Garbage 33

Evacuating for the Hurricane 34

You Can't Put the Red Sea in a Poem 36

Equanimity 37

Recipe 38

Christmas Tree Recycled in the Dunes 39

If you want to build a ship, don't drum up people together to collect wood and don't assign them tasks and work, but rather teach them to long for the endless immensity of the sea.
—Antoine de Saint-Exupéry

Sand Stories

Leave your dreams
in sand: sculptures
of sea turtles, sleeping unicorns.

Etch them with sharp
edges of shells—
love stories: Leigh and Lynn,

Happy Birthday Marcus.
Even as time vanishes
in the clean sweep of tide,

      Maria + Jason   forev

A Father Teaches His Daughter
to Ride the Waves

He carries her on his shoulders,
her fingers clasping the boogie board
he's taught her to steady over her head.
He wades out past the first foam
to where the blue deepens,
where she'll feel the thrill of the challenge
when she coasts back to shore.
He carried her
cradled in his quivering arms
when she was still wet
with vernix from the womb, carried her
when she cried, bewildered by her new world,
carried her in a backpack to the park
and the first time she saw the sea, carried her
with one arm, juggling groceries
 in the other, carried the tunes she loved
when he put her to bed,
carried her picture in his wallet
and her dreams on his chest, carried them
in his breath as he slept. He carries
all that still
as he lifts her onto the board,
gives a gentle push,
and releases her to the waves.

The Hunt

Walking along the shoreline
in January's cold clarity, my friend Sandy
spies a shark tooth, coveted treasure
of every beachcomber. Its smooth shine
catches her practiced eye.

She gives it to me, a novice
at these things, though my students
and I have read plenty about sharks,
how they occasionally mistake
a wave-riding human
for a creature of the sea, while we stalk
and slaughter millions of them, cut
prized fins from live bodies, toss
butchered remains into bloodied waves.

I tell her how eight-year-old Elmer cried,
That's not fair! No wonder they attack us!

Sandy thanks me for this shard of child sense
that hunts for justice through shifting shoals.
She tucks his words into her mind's pocket,
as I roll the hard edge of my fossil
between the warm fingers of my gloves.

Orange Butterflies/Orange Blossoms

They match
        the way lovers match,
  how lives blend into one
          another, how for one
              sunlit
                  moment
          you can't tell
                  wing from bloom

Rite of Passage

A handful of boys to men,
a herd, a flock, a quiver, a swarm,
red danger flag today, hurricane beyond the horizon,
foam chops, rip tides slash. They stand unsteadily
waist deep in waves, no surfers or beach dwellers these.
They punch, wrestle, jab each other. Head locks
and twists, unabashed animal play.
A band, a knot, an army, a pod. The youngest
encased in life jacket stands slightly apart,
tests the waters alone. The rest
a pride, a bevy, a gaggle, a shiver,
grab legs, torsos, roar and hoot as they drag each other
down, a rite of common contortions. Muscles gleam
against the sun, slender or stocky, they tease and throw
their willful weight around, uneven-footed, none nods
to the ocean's power. I can't stop watching them, tiny specks
in tumultuous sea. I can't stop thinking
about the men I love, the strength it takes to swim
out of the school, the yoke, the troop, the pack,
to fight the relentless pull

Bluefish Lane

The whole west side of the road
intentionally wild
protecting beach dwellers
from the munitions dump
across the river. No one tames
wax myrtle extending its long fingers
towards the street, leaving it to mingle
with sweetgum, oak, and the dead sticks
of something that rotted in last year's hurricane.
You can lean a long time brown and broken
in the woods
and no one denies you
your place

Words Matter: Choose Wisely

says the sign on the red and white cooler
in my neighbor's front yard. Kids on bikes,
curious walkers, tourists who wander off the beach
lift the creaky top. We find smooth stones,
egg-sized, still heavy with the mountain
they long ago deserted, each painted
with a word. Should I prop open my door
with *imagination,* anchor fly-away papers
with *song,* or ponder *oblivious* and *obvious*
as bookends? *Sunrise* could last all day
on the mantel, and I could fiddle with *detrimental*
in my jacket pocket without causing harm. Visitors
will surely depart with *dolphins*
nestled in duffle bags, a teenager will tuck *courage*
under her pillow. I choose *wisely,*
so *understanding* remains
for the home that needs it most.

Rescue

Wind scuttles a toddler's rubber ball
toward the waves' greedy fingers,
a globe-painted orb,

lush green continents, spinning oceans.
I block its path, toss it
to the child's eager arms.

I splash back
at the sea, *today*
I saved the world.

Waiting for the Coronavirus

Windows open
to emerald ocean,
French wine,
blueberry scones,
a long, well-
traveled marriage—
isolation often
uncluttered time.

Yet fickle
as a hurricane,
this silent stalker
swirls to strike
a glancing blow
or total devastation—
a coiled wind
constricting lungs,
breath left
with nowhere
to rise and fall.

Here,
where land loses
its steady footing,
the tide
tosses up
bits of iridescence
unmoored and broken,
but doesn't wash away
a fool's
longing
to control my own
ebb and flow.

The Mayor Supports Oil Drilling off Our Coast

Light from the movie screen
       propped against the garage door
              flickers over somber faces

of newcomers and friends
       leaning back on lawn chairs.
              We watch clips from the *Deepwater*

oil spill, tar balls turning beaches
       into ghost towns, a pelican draped
              in toxic slush. Each attempt to flutter

its own feathers drowns it farther
       in sticky filth. We fear what can't
              be seen: secret folds of coral

drenched beyond survival,
       single-celled authors of the food chain
              caught in algae-smothered webs.

We learn of destruction caused
       long before the drill: chants that
              dolphins sing to navigate the sea

confused by constant sonic booms
       pounding the ocean floor.
              Months later, we defeat the Mayor,

but the threat continues.
       We know we must be watchful.
              Startled on our seaside stroll

by sudden shadows thrown across the sand,
      we look up to a perfect pod
            of pelicans, swooping overhead.

Words

Words tumble
  like waves over rocks
      spraying hard edges
          of thought,

    leaving ideas

          slippery
            but
          shining

The Leap

Two lanky teenage girls from Unit 211
hurdle over the fence around the pool, undeterred
by the locked gate. They tell me that Rhonda,
the new condo manager, closed the pool this morning,
storm brewing. She doesn't know we savor
every anthills-bulging-through-cracked cement
inch of this place, we rush like five-year-olds
to the tippy-toe edge of the waves before we back off.
Some of us spent years, decades even, dreaming
of living where land concedes its splendor
to the sea, where we walk on white clouds
reflected in the skim of water just underfoot
at low tide. Harry Richards in 612 and I disagree
about almost everything—guns and abortion
and who's free in America—but passing in the parking lot
he shows me the photo he took today of a dolphin,
midair in a giant leap that looks like it will land on the sun.

After the House Fire

The man and woman escaped
only with their night clothes
and their terrier,

all other softness in their lives
now ashes sifting through lumps
of metal, misshapen and mangled,

even the red pickup's
useless black bones hang
from the skeleton of a garage

haunted by the trees—
gaping at lush summer lawns,
a carefully pruned row

of burnt orange evergreens
that mock their name,
ghostly neighbors

still erect with arms raised,
heads proud, soft needles
fossilized, refusing

to disintegrate, like the blue
couch and wedding photos
and the old man's boots.

The Senior Citizen and the Boy Scout

The Boy Scout by Troop 42's stand
at the fair, jumped up and ran
to help me lock my bike.
Truth is, I didn't want help. You see,
I'm 63 and quite able to pedal around town.
It wasn't his fault, the leader—behind the table—
egged him on. *Help her, Dan.*

I said, *I'm fine*
but the man insisted, and poor Dan
has learned to obey those commands.
I'm not the nimblest with my hands
through coils and key, but the way I see it,
if I do it more, I'll be better by 64.
I could've been gracious and agreed,
and everyone would've been set at ease—
except me.

Instead, in a tone that surely cast me
as a crusty old crone, I said, *I don't need
your help.* He backed off and I fiddled
with the lock until it caught. I walked away.

All day I replayed what I wish
I'd been mature enough to say:
*Thanks, I'll try myself
if I can. You're a kid,
I bet you understand.*

Still, couldn't the troop leader
have told that part to Dan?

America

a deep black bruise
  covers
    two thirds of the sky
      steadily
          spreading your way

             if you're bathed
               in sunlight, you can still
              believe
                 nothing's gonna
                     spoil your day.

Phone Conversation with My Husband about Our
Final Resting Places

Listen, I know you want your ashes tossed
into the Gulf at Galveston, and I'll be
at peace a mile out in the Atlantic,
but I'd still like to leave
some marker of my path on this earth.

So, let's invest in fish plates!
I saw them today lining the boardwalk,
the length of a footprint and barely
three inches wide at the belly,
black slate smartly adorned
with yellow letters. You know how sweet
the boardwalk is here
on this tiny North Carolina island—
no Atlantic City casinos in blazing lights
or corn dog stands flanking every step,
just five blocks of wooden planks
between guest cottages with geraniums
blooming in window boxes
and dunes that sweep towards the sea.

Yes, we get our choice of inscription,
(a fifty-character limit). Almost all
of the hundred or so already sunken
into the boards engrave *memory*—
happy memories here, in loving
memory, and who wouldn't remember
stepping off sand into foreverness,
curved rim of the horizon
all the cradle you need.

Hmm, I like that: *They loved
the ocean and it loved them back, love,
(each other's name).* The only thing is,
it's over the limit, and three *loves*
on a tiny bluefish's back will sink it for sure.

I knew you'd understand! No bones
buried under a private stone. Here we'll be
where everyone strolls in others' footsteps
to watch sea oats sway, feel
the ocean breathe, and hear gulls calling
all of our names.

Ghost Crabs on the Beach at Night

The sand stirs underfoot
    with the confluence
        of isopods and beach hoppers

        who weave their way
            beneath a skyful of stars
                and a misshapen moon

            that embraces them
                with just enough light
                    for their nightly work.

                But visitors shine
            their private moons,
        perfect flashlight circles

to tease ghost crabs
    who hunkered down all day
        in slanted tunnels, waiting

            for the cool safety of sundown
                to emerge from tiny holes,
                    and scavenge for survival.

                    Their startled bodies
                scamper away
            from the blinding beams,

        as humans
    with menacing eyes
haunt the dark.

Last Year for the Carnival at the Beach

Summer rolls out
on six truckloads
of pink and green dragons
with scooped seats,
blue horses and pink cats
with feathered caps and grinning faces
that don't wave
goodbye. Last year for the carnival.
Hello condos.
I'd wish the ghosts of purple dinosaurs
would hiss through the concrete
and haunt the new arrivals,
but you can't blame
people who won't even know
they've trampled magic
under their flip-flopped feet.

Garbage

Creepy old guy's digging through
the garbage at 6:00 am—
Bill complains
on the locals' page.
Neighbors suggest he's an artist,
gathering tin to shape
into tourist treasures,
replace *creepy*
with *harmless, quiet,*
down on luck,
vow to leave sorted cans
along his route, even say
his name.

Bill retorts *SO WHAT*
DO I TELL MY KIDS?
preparing for school
in morning shadows.

I reply:
Go to school, my dear ones,
learn to salvage
the bounty that belongs
to us all. Scrounge
through rubbish to find it,
don't be shooed away
like a swarming fly.
It's your world to retrieve.

Evacuating for the Hurricane

The day before, the waves spill
    the sea's incantation—*come rest*
      in this gentle promise,

      seagulls dismiss the ocean's
        song, fly towards the storm's eye
        to settle inside

        its womb and spiral where it wills them.
          Wingless, we will ride the other way,
          unencumbered

          like the birds, having learned to lean
            on lightness, only bearing
            my bag of journals,

      your ukulele, the Navajo sand painting
        that hangs above our bed—earth holding
        hands with sky,

      earrings from everywhere I've been,
        my hard-bound *Leaves of Grass,*
        spine half chewed

by my childhood dog, but no words
      lost. A week's worth of clothes. The rest
      replaceable,

we could start again with different pots.
    If we didn't find heavy cast iron,
      the lighter versions

are still dependable
      for sealing in the goodness
           of what serves us well.

You Can't Put the Red Sea in a Poem

a famous poet warned. If you let it in, your poem is crammed
with two million Israelites clutching babies in arms,
with satchels of clothes and unleavened bread,
and you've invited in the enormous weight of a God
who punishes evil by slaying slave owners' children,
so here come the Egyptians as God splits open
that unmentionable sea just in time
for the migrants to cross and closes it right up
on the pursuers, and your poem is choking on all those
drowning men, flailing horses and wrecked chariots,
and next thing you know you have races and nations and power
and poverty all spilled in the red ink of misery
and your poem is overwhelmed—
it's baffled that He (since it's always he) never sat them all down
and explained this wasn't what He had in mind
those intense seven days he created a world so magnificent
poets can't stop trying to describe it, which is what happened
to me when it snowed at the beach at high tide, not just a dusting
but a full-on onslaught of snow we hadn't seen
in these parts in years, downing telephone wires
and snapping tree branches and power out.
When the snow finally stopped and the tide receded,
it left a wide strip of sand along the shore, snow mounds piled
like crystal dunes on one side and the ocean's perpetual roar
on the other, and in between—the tiny miracle
of a parting I passed through, kicking scattered seashells
like nothing strange and beautiful had happened,
nothing that needs to mention the Red Sea.

Equanimity

There are slow hinges on the kitchen cabinets
so the doors never slam. But I slam many doors

when my worries become unhinged. Then I slide
open the screen door and walk out to the ocean.

It urges me to listen
between roar and purr, abandon

my frantic grip trying to steer the tide.
I scroll my fingers over the smooth shell

that rests in my pocket, savor
the slippery sea inside my palm.

Recipe

We know each other,
morning's first beach walkers,
gawking at the crimson egg
that hovers on horizon's edge.

We stop to watch it crack,
yolk spreading across the sky,
nourishing us more than anything
scrambled up in kitchens.

No names, addresses,
loves, longings, losses.
We simply share this recipe
for how to start the day.

Christmas Tree Recycled in the Dunes

With thanks to the Cape Fear Surfrider Foundation

Stripped of angels
that haloed its crown, the tree
lies bare and awkward, shaved trunk
shoved into sparse remains of a dune lost
to last year's storms. Tourists laugh at its odd,
prone position, but soon its parched arms catch
swirls of sand and settle them gently on the rising
slope. The tree blends with beach elder and sea
oats, mingles with dwarf fountain grass
to become the dune's spine, its fragile
hold on integrity. Grown from the
deep emerald energy of the forest
the tree shines as the graced
do, even now reimagined.

About the Author

Joanne Durham is a retired educator living on the North Carolina coast, with the ocean as her backyard. She has loved poetry since she devoured the pages of *The Golden Treasury of Poetry* as a child. She is the author of *To Drink from a Wider Bowl,* winner of the 2021 Sinclair Prize (Evening Street Press 2022). She won the 2021 Prime 53 Poem Summer Challenge and was a finalist for the NC Poetry Society's Poet Laureate Award, the NC State Poetry Contest, and *Ruminate's* Broadside Prize. Her poetry has appeared or is forthcoming in numerous journals, including *Poetry East, Calyx, Third Wednesday, One Art, Juniper Poetry Journal, Quartet, Rise-Up Review, Pensive, Kosmos Quarterly, Love in the Time of COVID Chronicle, and Gyroscope.* She is an Associate Editor for *Evening Street Review.* When she's not immersed in poetry, Joanne practices yoga, plays tennis, delights in her grandchildren, and works for a better world for them to grow up in. For more about her background and poetry, see https://www.joannedurham.com/.

www.ingramcontent.com/pod-product-compliance
Lightning Source LLC
Chambersburg PA
CBHW031009090426
42737CB00008B/743